Homemade
Christmas
& Festive
Decorations

Collins

Homemade
Christmas & Festive
Decorations
25 home craft projects

Ros Badger with Elspeth Thompson
Photography by Benjamin J Murphy

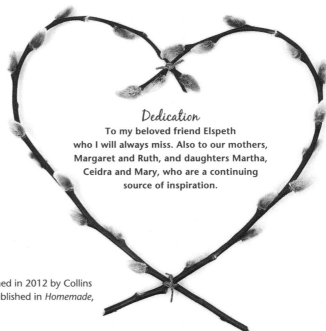

Dedication

**To my beloved friend Elspeth
who I will always miss. Also to our mothers,
Margaret and Ruth, and daughters Martha,
Ceidra and Mary, who are a continuing
source of inspiration.**

This paperback edition published in 2012 by Collins includes some material first published in *Homemade*, first published in 2009.

HarperCollins*Publishers*
77–85 Fulham Palace Road
London W6 8JB

www.harpercollins.co.uk

16 15 14 13 12

9 8 7 6 5 4 3 2 1

A catalogue record for this book is available from the British Library.

ISBN: 978-000-748955-8

Photography Benjamin J Murphy

Editors Emma Callery and Sarah Tomley

Design Tracy Killick

Illustrations Mary Mathieson and Peter Liddiard

Packager Tracy Killick Art Direction and Design

Printed and bound in China by South China Printing Co Ltd

Contents

Introduction

A homemade Christmas, or indeed any festivity, must be the most rewarding way to celebrate. Making something for someone else with love – whether it is a cake, a Christmas wreath or a simple greetings card – feels good, and in a world often said to be divided between those who spend money in order to save time and those who spend time in order to save money, our time is still seen as the ultimate luxury.

It is not a cliché that Christmas is about giving and there are plenty of ideas in this book that would make wonderful gifts. Mostly, however, this is a book about how to dress your home to create a beautiful, warm and inspiring environment in which to welcome friends and family to celebrate events throughout the year. All of the projects have been chosen because they can be imbued with meaning, in a way that's simply not possible for mass-made products – you can incorporate favourite old items that have seen better days or have long been outgrown but retain fond memories. These decorations can also be made without too much expense and uniquely tailored to suit a loved one or friend. There is nothing more rewarding and nurturing for the soul than spending time making something that is genuinely appreciated and admired by others.

This book is filled with ideas, many of them very simple and quick to make. We hope they will not only enhance your celebrations and save you money, but also help you recycle – and upcycle – materials that you may already have lying around.

I am forever encouraging people to get into the habit of keeping old wrapping paper, cards, ribbons, fabric scraps, buttons and yarn, not in a post-war 'make do and mend' way, but because much of today's wasted material can be made into very stylish new objects. There has never been so much 'stuff' around – so don't waste it, grab it with both hands! Look out for interesting items that other people don't spot. Once you have got used to noticing pretty old buttons on flea-market jackets and the beautiful paper someone used for your own birthday presents, you'll begin to see just how much wonderful stuff is there for the

taking. Save what you can and it will give you an endless source of materials to turn into beautiful creations of your own.

We have created a wide range of projects, which will allow readers to use even the most basic of craft skills in new and unusual ways. There are plenty of ideas and alternatives for the skilled maker as well as the reader who feels more at home with a glue stick than a sewing needle.

I have always been proud to be seen as a creative person, but now we are firmly back to a time where craft is not the preserve of an envied talented few, but widespread across the globe. 'Homemade' (including 'homegrown') has become a way of life for a huge number of people. So many can now be heard saying with pride, 'I made it myself!' People are no longer happy with doing an occasional piece of knitting on their commuter train or taking a homemade gift to a party – they want to 'live the life', embracing the authenticity and love behind everything homemade.

This book is for anyone seeking respite from impersonal commercialism and all things disposable, and who would like to spend half an hour or so now and then making things – either alone, or with friends or family. Enjoy the process and reap the rewards.

Ros Badger

Christmas

Dressing the Christmas tree

Dressing the Christmas tree is a lovely ritual in which all the family can participate. Choose a time when you can work in an unhurried way – ideally towards the end of the afternoon or early evening so that the lights can be switched on with a degree of ceremony when it gets dark.

The idea of the 'styled' tree, with all the objects newly bought to fit in with an agreed colour scheme, is anathema to the homemade approach. Instead, bring out vintage decorations that have become family heirlooms since your own childhood and beyond, plus newer ones made by hand, perhaps some of them by the children in your life. Homemade items bring an energy all of their own to the tree, adding to its significance as a family talisman, loaded with memories and associations, from year to year.

Like the eggs on the Easter tree (see page 44), your collection of homemade tree decorations will become a treasured possession that you can add to year by year. As well as making pieces, such as the embroidered felt shapes on the next page, we also buy a few new or second-hand items every so often – from vintage finds on eBay to those picked up on trips around the country or travels abroad.

Less is most definitely less when it comes to tree decoration. In our book, you can't have enough decorations and we load our trees with this eclectic mix of old and new until there is very little greenery showing in between.

Felt decorations

Bursting with cheerful colour and homespun charm, these felt decorations couldn't be simpler, and they are a great way of involving children in pre-Christmas preparations.

You will need

- Felt, which is generally much cheaper when sold by the metre than in smaller squares
- Ribbon (ideally recycled lengths from your stash of ribbons)
- Sewing threads in contrasting colours to felt
- Sequins (optional)

To make a felt decoration

• Using a paper pattern only where really necessary (there are templates on pages 82–83 for the decorations shown here), cut out the decorations, using two layers of felt for each one. For the heart, you could cut out some of the pieces of felt using pinking shears to add a pretty, zig-zag edging.

• Sew the pieces together by stitching around the edge in tiny running stitches. Use a contrasting colour to add some basic but attractive decoration. Secure a loop of pretty ribbon at the top edge as you are sewing.

Star, heart and stocking decorations

• These three lovely decorations are shown below right. We used chain stitch to decorate the star, heart and stocking with words.

• For the stocking, use the template on page 83. Start by attaching some white felt (the cuff) to each piece of red by working a row of chain stitch across the bottom edge of the white cuff. Then stitch the red pieces together by sewing around the outer edges in running stitch, but leave the top open. Attach the ribbon loop to the corner of the top back edge. Work a row of running stitches across the top of each side of the stocking to secure the white cuff. There should be plenty of space for a chocolate!

Bauble decoration

• Cut out two circles freehand or use the template on page 82. Join the circles by sewing around the outside with running stitch, leaving a space about 2cm (¾in) wide to add stuffing.

• After stuffing with kapok (toy stuffing) or a clean pair of tights, continue sewing up the gap with running stitch, adding the ribbon loop for hanging.

Holly decoration

• Use the templates on page 82. Cut out two pieces of green felt using the leaf template, and sew veins onto them using small back stitches. Cut out two or three red berries using the berry template, and stitch to the top near the ribbon. Sew the leaves together, sewing in a loop at the top.

Adding sequins

• We sewed sequins to the bauble and Christmas tree. Using a continuous thread, add the sequins randomly all over the decoration. Or you could add the sequins before stitching the felt pieces together.

Knitted angel

Placing the angel at the top of the Christmas tree is traditionally the final task in the annual ritual of decorating the branches. And what could be more charming than this little knitted angel?

You will need

- 4-ply wool in the following colours (use up ends to make this angel as it takes tiny amounts): cream, tan or skin tone, pink, yellow (or other colour, for hair)
- 3.25mm (UK size 10; US size 12) knitting needles
- Stuffing or cotton wool

Tension over stocking stitch
14sts and 18 rows = 5cm (2in)

Abbreviations
See page 81

Arms (make 2)
Cast on 10sts in cream, 2sts in tan.
Work 6 rows in stocking st (knit one row, purl one row).
Cast off 12sts.

The arms and legs naturally roll so that the reverse side of st st is on the outside. Catch together cast-on edge to cast-off edge in the direction that they have rolled. Sew in any loose ends.

Legs (make 2)
Cast on 12sts in tan, 2sts in pink or a contrast colour.
Work 6 rows stocking st.
Cast off 14sts.
Catch and sew edges as for the arms.

Body
Cast on 20sts in cream.
Work 17 rows in st st.
Then knit 6 rows more.
Cast off.

Head
Cast on 4sts in tan or skin tone.
Row 1: Knit.
Row 2: Purl.
Row 3: Knit, inc 1st at either end of row (6sts).
Row 4: Purl.
Repeat rows 3 and 4 (8sts).
Work 4 rows more in stocking st.
Row 11: Knit, dec 1st at either end of row (6sts).

Continues on page 17

Row 12: Purl.
Rows 13 & 14: As rows 10 and 11 (4sts).
Row 15: Purl.
Row 16: Knit.
Cast off.

Wings (make 2)

Wings are all garter st (knit every row).
Cast on 6sts in cream.
Rows 1 & 2: Knit.
Row 3: Knit, inc 1st at either end of row (10sts).
Row 4: Cast on 4sts at beginning of row, knit to end (14sts).
Rows 5–7: Work 3 rows in garter st.
Rows 8–11: Rep last 4 rows (18sts).
Row 12: Cast on 4sts at beginning of row, knit to end (22sts).
Row 13: Knit, dec 1st at beg of row.
Row 14: Knit, dec 1st at end of row.
Row 15: Knit, dec 1st at beginning of row (19sts).
Cast off (this is the outside edge of your wing).

Skirt

Cast on 44sts in cream and knit 2 rows.
Row 3: Knit.
Row 4: Purl.
Rows 5–18: Rep rows 3 and 4, ending on a purl row.
Row 19: K4, k2tog, * k3, k2tog, rep from * 6 times more, k3 (36sts).
Row 20: Purl.
Row 21: K3, k2tog, * k2, k2tog, rep from * 6 times more, k3 (28sts).
Row 22: Purl.
Row 23: K2, k2tog, * k1, k2tog, rep from * 6 times more, k3 (20sts).
Row 24: Purl.
Cast off.
Fold in half and sew the side seam of the skirt.

To make up

• For the head, sew the side seams, then stuff from base. Embroider eyes with two small over stitches (see page 79) for each.

• To make hair, thread a darning needle with yellow (or any preferred colour) yarn and stitch around the head with random running stitch (see page 79) but leaving loops instead of pulling the yarn flat.

• For the body, fold in half and catch the legs at each corner of the cast-on edge and sew across with running stitch, securing the legs in position as you sew. Sew the side seam of the body, then stuff the body and sew approximately 5mm (¼in) either side on cast-off edge for shoulders.

• Attach the base of the head to the 'neck' space, using over stitch or any neat stitch as preferred.

• Place the skirt over the doll's body and use over stitch to catch the cast-off edge around the body approximately 1cm (½in) below the garter st detail of the body.

• Sew in any loose ends.

• To attach the wings, sew the cast-on edge of each wing to the centre back of the angel's body.

Tips

This pattern can also be adapted to make little dolls for children – just leave out the wings and change the colours of the dress. Small items such as this are great for using up any scraps of wool left from other creative projects.

Floating baubles

Silver and crystal baubles are amazing at reflecting light. Hang a group of them above candles on the kitchen table for a decoration that's a blaze of light glittering on surfaces.

You will need

- Clear fishing line or invisible thread
- 2 small carpet tacks or short nails
- Hammer
- Selection of silver or crystal Christmas decorations

To make

- Attach the two tacks to walls either side of your table, then stretch a piece of fishing line or invisible thread between the tacks, so it reaches from one wall to another. Make sure the line is tight and well secured at either end as the weight of the baubles may stretch the line and cause it to sag.

- Hang the decorations above the table by tying a length of fishing line or invisible thread to each bauble and hanging them at different heights from the stretched length of fishing line.

- Place small candles or nightlights below the baubles and light them. Enjoy the view!

Tips

This idea can be adapted to use any groups of coordinated decorations, even paper baubles or small pompoms (see page 66), but make sure they hang well away from the candles. Ask your children to make some little trinkets to hang over the candles, and hang them alone or among glittering baubles. Children really enjoy seeing their work go centre-stage, especially at Christmas.

Groups of items on wire, line or thread make great decorations all round the house. A natural selection – using items such as fir cones, leaves, dried orange segments, cinnamon sticks and thistles – looks wonderful hanging across a window, especially if you lightly spray the elements with glitter and hang them from the line using festive ribbons.

Festive mantelpiece

There are all sorts of fancy Christmas decorations for sale in the shops, but to our mind, nothing can beat the traditional favourites, especially a holly and ivy garland over a roaring fire.

To decorate the mantelpiece

• Clear and dust your shelf or mantelpiece, then drape the ivy in swags, anchoring the pieces with the heavier sprigs of holly and punctuating with fir cones, bright berries and other natural objects.

• Weave a set of fairy lights in among the foliage – plain white or red chilli pepper lights look wonderful at Christmas.

• Add a few baubles, other special decorations or cards as you like. It can be nice to give homemade cards some recognition by displaying them in a prominent place, as shown below.

• A real fire in the grate is the true finishing touch. If you have one, stack plenty of wood alongside it for a feeling of warmth and security, whatever the weather. For Christmas, you might like to track down some apple or pear wood, both of which burn with a gloriously atmospheric scent.

Tips

The garland doesn't have to be made of ivy – pine, holly leaves or any evergreen will do. To decorate stairs, tie the evergreen and baubles to some thin rope using twine or wire.

You will need

• Trailing ivy (can be freshly pruned from the garden or bought from a florist)

• Sprigs of holly

• Fir cones, berries and other woodland items, perhaps gathered on a winter's walk

• Set of fairy lights

• Baubles and other favourite decorations

Christmas wreath

This naturally beautiful festive wreath is a far cry from the tinselly versions available in shops and markets. It is also surprisingly fun and easy to make, and will be much admired on your front door.

You will need

- Whippy willow branches
- Trailing ivy
- Roll of florists' wire
- Holly leaves
- Holly or other red berries
- Fir cones
- Mossy twigs
- Hydrangea flowerhead – the redder the better
- Strong ribbon or string for hanging

To make

- Lay out the whippy willow branches in a circle to the desired circumference for your wreath. Lay long strands of ivy on top of it and lash all layers tightly together with the florists' wire to make a long 'sausage' of foliage. This gives your wreath a good solid base and will help keep a strong round shape. (It's possible to use holly and ivy alone as a base, but you may find that the weight of larger wreaths will cause them to stretch into an oval when hanging.)

- Form the sausage into a wreath shape and secure the ends together with wire. This makes the base of the wreath.

- Working around the wreath, evenly attach your decorations – holly leaves, berries, cones, twigs, sections from the hydrangea head and any other Christmassy foliage – around the circumference, securing each one with the florists' wire.

- When you have worked once around, hang the wreath to view from a distance, and continue to add more leaves and berries if any section looks sparse.

- Attach a length of strong ribbon or string at the top rear of the wreath where it will not show, for tying around a nail or hook on your door.

- The wreath should last around three weeks if hanging outside and may even dry out sufficiently to carry on as an indoor decoration, to be supplemented with seasonal flowers and foliage throughout the rest of the year.

Tips

For the cheapest, greenest and most natural effect, forage your own foliage from your garden or a hedgerow. Or take an early-morning trip to a flower market where the foliage will be fresh, and buy enough to supply a few like-minded friends too.

Cranberry Christmas decorations

Cranberries have a rich wine colour and lovely plump shape that makes them a wonderful alternative to shop-bought decorations. They traditionally symbolise peace and the earth's abundance.

You will need
- Cranberries
- Darning needle
- String and/or florists' wire

Cranberry hearts, circles and stars

- Use florists' wire or a malleable alternative that will hold its shape to thread together a short length of cranberries.

- Twist the two ends of wire together and shape into a heart, circle, star or any festive shape that takes your fancy.

- Attach a length of ribbon or string and hang your decoration on the tree, door handles or wall during the Christmas season.

Cranberry garland (see page 28)

- The simplest way to use cranberries as a decoration is to thread them onto thin twine or coloured string using a darning needle.

- Thread the needle with twine and tie a large knot at one end, then begin threading the fruit, pushing the needle through the fruit from side to side, rather than top to bottom.

- When your garland is long enough, tie another knot to finish.

Tips

Cranberry decorations will keep for year after year, but remember that the berries will shrink as they dry and you will need to tighten them slightly on the wire or twine. The berries are unlikely to be completely dry by twelfth night, so leave them for a few days in a warm space such as an airing cupboard, then carefully pull the string or wire through the dry fruit to make the garland or decoration more compact.

You could also use the wire method to make a small wreath for hanging on the front door. The berries will last longer outside but note that if they freeze they will disintegrate as they thaw, so bring the wreath inside on freezing nights if possible.

If you have any cranberries left, place some in the base of a jam jar and stand a white candle among them for a festive table decoration.

Christmas card garland

Christmas cards can be recycled as pretty labels for gifts, but they can also be cut and stitched into colourful baubles to make an original festive garland. This really is a perfect example of reduce, recycle, reuse.

You will need

• 6cm (2¾in) biscuit cutter or circular stencil
• Lots of old Christmas cards
• Pen or pencil
• Sharp scissors
• Sewing thread

To make

• Using a pencil, draw around your biscuit cutter or stencil on the back of each card, making as many circles as you need. The decoration works best if double-sided, so measure the length of garland you need, the number of circles needed to achieve this, and then cut double that number of circles. Think about where you are positioning the stencil on each card to make the most of your patterns.

• Set up your sewing machine with a coloured thread that suits your scheme, and stitch a length of thread around 20cm (8in) long. Then take two circles of card, hold them wrong sides together, and sew through the centre. As you reach the edge, add another pair of circles and repeat this until you have used up all your cards.

• Continue stitching another 20cm (8in) of thread only, then cut the thread. Hang your garland wherever you need a touch of Christmas colour.

Tips

Any printed or plain paper could be adapted to make a garland like this – you could even use type-printed pages from an old paperback. We sometimes make smaller versions of these and send them as homemade Christmas cards.

Hand-painted Christmas plate

Many people collect traditional Christmas plates, marked with the year of production to remember past festivities. Why not start a new tradition by painting a festive one yourself each year?

You will need

- A plate (we used vintage plates from a charity shop)
- A large piece of paper
- Ceramic paint
- Ceramic painting pen (optional)
- Paint brushes

To make

• Draw around your plate onto paper. If you're using a vintage plate with a pattern, draw the outline of this on the paper too. Then draw your own pattern onto the paper, keeping it as simple as possible at this stage, and add the year of production.

• Copy your pattern onto the plate using a fine paintbrush and ceramic paint (and pen, if using one). Work slowly. If you make a mistake, simply wipe the plate clean with a kitchen sponge and start again.

• When you are happy with your design, bake the plate in the oven for 30 minutes at approximately 180°C (350°F), Gas 4. (This may vary – check the individual instructions on your ceramic paints.)

Tips

Asking your children to paint a plate every year is a great way to celebrate their creative achievements. Or you could all paint it together, making it a traditional family event every December. Ceramic paint and pens are readily available at craft shops and are both reasonably priced and long lasting, but you could opt to spend time at a cosy ceramics café where they will provide all sorts of pottery shapes for decoration.

Advent calendar

Made from an old linen sheet with 24 hand-painted pockets, this beautiful advent calendar is reusable year after year, and has the scope to become a much-treasured family heirloom.

You will need

- An old sheet, or plain linen or cotton fabric at least 82 x 125cm (32 x 50in). If buying from a new 90cm- (36in-) wide fabric, buy a length of 125cm (50in)
- Fabric paints and fabric crayons
- Assorted cotton threads for machine sewing
- Piece of dowelling approximately 76cm (30in)
- Ribbon for hanging

To make

- From the fabric, cut a piece measuring 74 x 82cm (29 x 32in). Then cut out 23 smaller pieces of various sizes for the pockets as given below.

Six pieces at each of the following sizes:
11 x 11cm (4¼ x 4¼in)
11 x 13cm (4¼ x 5in)
12 x 12cm (4¾ x 4¾in)

Five pieces measuring:
13 x 15cm (5 x 6in)

One piece measuring:
15 x 15cm (6 x 6in) for the central 'Christmas Eve' pocket.

- Using the fabric paints and fabric crayons, decorate each piece with a number from 1 to 23 and add some Christmas images, if you like. You could take inspiration from favourite cards or images from the internet. Decorate the largest piece – 15 x 15cm (6 x 6in) – with a special image for Christmas Eve. We painted an angel.

- Make sure to leave at least 1cm (½in) around the image on all sides for hemming and attaching to the background.

- When all the small pieces are decorated, fold over 1cm (½in) along the top of each one, press with an iron, then hem this top edge with a contrasting-coloured thread. We chose a zig-zag stitch on the sewing machine from the embroidery settings, and it looks very effective (see right). You might find other possibilities.

- Carefully fold in the three other sides on each piece by 1cm (½in) and iron to hold the fold in place. The pieces are then ready to attach to the large background fabric.

- Pin each pocket randomly onto the large piece, mixing up the

numbers however you like. Then sew around the three folded sides of each pocket to secure them to the backing using a standard machine running stitch. Make sure you leave the top edge unsewn.

- When all 24 pockets are attached, fold over 1cm (½in) all around the main piece and iron to hold. Then fold over another 1cm (½in) on the two side and bottom edges. Sew around these three sides with the same stitch and coloured thread used to hem the pocket tops (our red zig-zag stitch).

- To make the channel at the top for hanging, fold over the top edge by 2cm (¾in) and sew across using a decorative stitch (our red zig-zag stitch). Thread the dowelling through the channel, attach the ribbon to either end and hang in position ready to fill with goodies for the days leading up to Christmas Eve.

Tips

This is a project a whole family or school class could work on together – each person choosing a number of pockets to decorate. Or you could do as we did and ask a talented friend (in our case the artist Mary Mathieson) to paint the entire design.

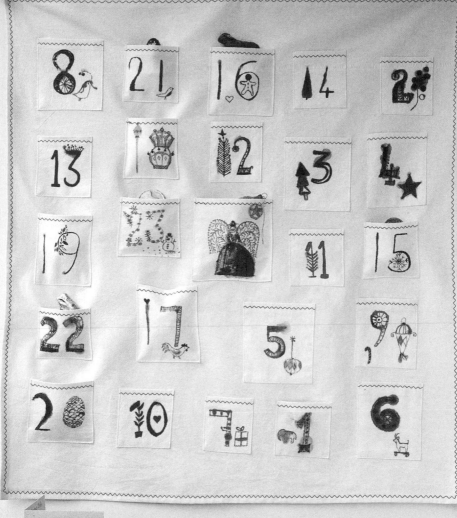

Christmas stocking

You can often find winter wool blankets in faded rose, cream or blue or earthy tones of brown and grey in charity shops. They make lovely baby blankets and cushions, but are truly fabulous as Christmas stockings.

You will need

- Old wool blanket or piece of linen large enough for the size stocking you want
- Embroidery needle
- Embroidery thread or knitting yarn

To make

- Draw a simple stocking shape onto paper (newspaper or lining paper are also good for this) to the size you want, using the template on page 83.

- Fold your fabric in half and pin your stocking shape onto it, thinking about where you want any stripes or patterns to appear on the stocking. You'll be cutting two pieces at once, so if you want to select two particular pieces of fabric or match stripes, you may need to cut each piece individually. If the blanket has stitched or ribbon edging you could incorporate this at the top of your stocking (as we did with the one shown here).

- Decide what you would like to embroider onto your fabric and whether you want to decorate both sides of the stocking. Names are a good option, as are words like Noël, Happy Christmas and Peace. Traditional Christmas images – such as Christmas trees, snowflakes, stars and hearts – look beautiful when chain stitched onto wool. We used a Scandinavian image of a bird (see template on page 83). There are lots of free patterns on the internet to inspire you. Use simple

stitches (see pages 78–79) and embroidery thread or yarn split into two (to achieve the right thickness).

- When you have decorated your stocking place the wrong sides together, pin in place and blanket stitch (see page 79) all around.

- Finish by sewing a ribbon loop onto the back corner of the stocking for hanging.

Tips

If you are embroidering or adding appliqué to both sides, face the toes towards each other so that you don't end up with your hard work on the wrong side of one of the pieces. This idea works equally well with vintage linen and is another perfect way to use small pieces of pretty fabrics.

Valentine's Day

Rose-scented Valentine heart

A patchwork, sweet-scented heart is a lasting way to say 'I love you' on Valentine's day. This one draws upon the Elizabethan tradition of rose pot pourri to create a heady, romantic scent.

You will need

- Fresh roses
- Baking tray
- Fresh or dried lavender (or orris root)
- A teaspoon or two of spice (cinnamon, cloves or nutmeg are traditional)
- Rose essential oil

To make the pot pourri

- Using fresh red roses, wait until the flowers are fully opened before harvesting the petals. Lay them out on a baking tray or flat sheet and place them somewhere warm for several days to dry out.

- Fill a jam jar with the dried petals, and add a tablespoon of dried lavender or dried orris root (available from health food shops), which acts as a fixative.

- Add a teaspoon or two of fresh cinnamon, cloves or nutmeg – or any other spice you like – then shake the jar gently to mingle the ingredients.

- Add 5 drops of the wonderful rose essential oil.

- Seal the lid and leave for 10 days, shaking the jar every couple of days.

To make the heart

- Stitch together some scraps of fabric with romantic associations – from some favourite old shirts, for instance – and cut out two heart shapes.

- With right sides facing, sew the fabric pieces together, leaving a small gap of around 3cm (1in). Turn the fabric pieces right sides out through the gap and use plain or fancy traditional stitches to decorate the seams.

- Stuff the heart with rose pot pourri and stitch to close the gap.

Tip

You can mingle the pot pourri with dried rice to make it stretch further and to give the heart more weight.

Valentine paper cut-out

Traditional paper cutting is called *scherenschnitte* – look up this term or 'paper cutting' online and you will find hundreds of visual references for incredible patterns. We have made two paper-cut valentines here that could be used to decorate a wall or table for Valentine's Day or posted as special valentine tokens.

If you don't feel confident about your drawing skills, start by drawing a simple heart (see the template on page 84) with an arrow through it and write your loved one's name or a love message across the centre. Alternatively use one of the many free stencils that are available on internet blogs for downloading. Remember that although paper cutting works well on plain paper, it also lends itself beautifully to patterned papers, particularly those with Japanese designs.

Paper cutting is easier than it looks and requires very few tools – a sharp pair of scissors, a craft knife and some thin card. It goes without saying that the more complicated the design the longer it will take to produce, but anyone can make a simple cut-out, and part of the attraction is the naivety of this process – think of all the paper snowflakes we made as children.

Relax and have fun. Your lines don't have to be straight and the curves can be a bit wobbly. With practice, you may surprise yourself and end up producing something as complex and gorgeous as the most beautiful traditional designs.

Tip
If you make an especially wonderful cut-out and are proud of your production, you could frame it and give it away as a birthday present, or start a collection to add to each year.

Valentine bed garland

This pretty garland is a great way to show your love and appreciation and will make any setting immediately more romantic. A short version makes a wonderful valentine gift and card – it's a perfect couple.

You will need
- Red felt
- Red sewing thread
- Red rose petals (optional)

To make
- Using the template on page 84 cut out as many red hearts as you can from the felt you have. (We cut out around 50.)

- Thread your sewing machine with red sewing thread and stitch without any fabric for approximately 20cm (8in), then stitch across your first heart. Stitch without any fabric for another 5cm (2in) or so before you sew the second heart, then continue like this until all the hearts are joined together.

- To finish, keep sewing for a further 20cm (8in) before you cut the thread. The thread at each end will allow you to attach the garland to a bed or a wall, but you could simply lay it across a table for a romantic dinner *à deux*, or run it across your pillows or sofa.

Tips
If you don't want to use felt, any firm red fabric will do, but don't use anything that will fray because the joy of this garland is that it doesn't need hemming. You could even use red card or paper, or a cut-out of a printed romantic poem. If you have lots of time and can crochet, you could make a collection of hearts and join them together with chain stitch. We collected red rose petals and lay these in the shape of a heart in front of the garland (see left). This would work equally well on a floor or table, and combined with the garland makes a truly romantic setting.

Easter

Easter tree

Hanging hand-decorated eggs on branches of spring leaves and blossom is a lovely tradition that can become part of family life. You can use a mixture of old and new hand-painted eggshells.

You will need

- Raw eggs
- Empty egg box
- Darning needle
- Vinegar
- Paints, felt pens, pastels, glue, paper and fabric scraps – whatever comes to hand for decorating
- Food colouring
- Ribbon or fine cord with beads
- Small branches for the 'tree'

To make

- To blow a raw egg, place it upright in the egg box and use a darning needle to make a small hole in the top. Turn the egg carefully upside down and make a slightly larger hole in the bottom. Break up the yolk by poking the needle about inside, and then gently, but steadily, blow into the smaller hole to evacuate the innards into a bowl (save for making scrambled eggs or pancakes).

- Rinse the egg by submerging the shell in water with a little vinegar added and blowing out again. Allow to dry.

- Now you're ready to decorate. You can paint eggshell with poster paints, felt pens or pastels, and your designs might be anything from free-form flowers, chicks and rabbits to polka dots, stripes, spirals or patterns that run around the circumference of the shell. You can also stick on paper, fabric, pressed or imitation flowers or other shapes – adding ribbons, bows or other ornamentation as the fancy takes you.

- To attach the eggs to the tree, cut a length of ribbon and glue it carefully right around the egg lengthways, tying the free ends into a bow at the top.

- Alternatively, thread one end of a fine cord or ribbon through the darning needle and tie a knot in the other end. Thread a small bead onto the cord or ribbon and pass the needle through the large hole at the base of the egg and out through the smaller hole at the top. The bead should then anchor the cord or ribbon in place, allowing you to make a loop for tying at the top of the egg.

- After Easter, store the eggs in the empty egg box in a safe place until next year.

Tips

A naturally blue eggshell makes a pretty background. Or you can dye white ones: add a few drops of food colouring to a pan of water with the eggshells and simmer for 10 minutes.

Easter egg bunting

This quick and simple Easter bunting uses saved, vintage wrapping paper with Easter themes, but pale blue, rose, lemon or cream paper will give you a refreshing, natural look that's perfect for welcoming the spring.

You will need

- Several pieces of wrapping paper, old or new
- Stiff paper or card
- Darning needle
- Fishing line or invisible thread

To make

- Cut out an egg-shaped stencil using the template on page 84. Using a pencil, draw around the stencil onto the back of the paper or card you are using, making as many ovals as you need. This decoration works best if double-sided, so measure the length of bunting you want and work out the number of ovals you need to achieve this – allowing for a reasonable amount of space between them. Then cut double that number of shapes. Think about where you are positioning the stencil on the paper or card to make the most of your patterns.

- Glue together your ovals, so each 'egg' has a pretty pattern on both sides.

- Thread a darning needle with fishing line (or a sewing needle with invisible thread). Tie a knot around 20cm (8in) from the end, so you will have a long, free piece of line or thread at the end to hang the bunting. Then start threading your eggs onto the line or thread, knotting each one into place as you go, and allowing space between each egg.

- When you reach the last egg, knot the thread and then allow around 20cm (8in) of line or thread before cutting it. Hang your bunting inside or outside, on a sunny day.

Tips

Wallpaper also works well for this bunting. If you have time, you could paint designs onto card and cut them out for the egg shapes, or even make some paper cut-outs (see page 38). You could also add sequins, stickers or fresh or dried flowers or petals. If you don't have a sewing machine or just prefer not to sew your eggs together, simply punch two holes at the narrower end of each egg and thread through a piece of ribbon or string.

Easter bird decorations

Easter tables look lovely topped with painted eggs dangling from a blossom branch, but this is a refreshing alternative that allows for greater creativity. It's also simple enough for children to make.

You will need

- Felt for 1 bird and 3 eggs, plus scraps for decorating
- 60cm (24in) length of ribbon or tape
- Sequins or anything else you fancy for decorating the birds and eggs

To make

- Cut out 2 felt pieces for the bird and 6 egg shapes, using the bird and egg templates on page 84.

- Decorate each side of the pieces. Face the birds towards each other on the table to make sure the wings will be attached to the correct side for sewing together later. Sew a wing to the facing side of each bird and embroider an eye with satin stitch or any simple stitch. When decorating the eggs, we attached and embroidered a simple bird onto one egg, a felt flower shape and a small heart to the second, and sequins to the third, but anything goes here, so feel free to add whatever you want.

- Fold one end of the ribbon to make a loop and stitch this into place. For added decoration you could sew through a sequin or button to join the loop.

- Sandwich the ribbon between the two pieces of your first egg, then pin it in place. Sew around the egg with blanket or running stitch.

- Repeat the process for each motif, placing them around 9cm (3½in) apart.

- For the last egg, catch the end of the ribbon and tuck it between the egg pieces.

Tip

You can make your decoration any length and have any number of birds and eggs on it, but make sure you have enough ribbon before you start.

Pin the egg on the chicken

This delightful painted banner is a variation on the game 'pin the tail on the donkey'. It can be brought out every year for Easter parties or spring birthdays and doubles up as a game and decoration.

You will need

- A plain cotton or linen sheet
- Washable paints or inks
- Assortment of paintbrushes
- Stiff paper or card
- Sticky tape
- A blindfold

To make

- Using the sheet as your canvas, apply your design with the washable paints or inks. There are lots of tips online for copying and transferring pictures or designs onto fabric if you don't feel confident about painting freehand, or you could ask a talented friend or child to draw the pictures for you.

- While the banner is drying, draw around 10 egg shapes onto the paper or card, paint in an assortment of egg colours and cut out when dry. Just before you play the game, add a loop of sticky tape to the back of each egg for attaching it to the banner. This is the safest way for children to stick their eggs on the chicken.

To play

- Hang the banner against a wall or from the branches of a low-growing tree – we pegged ours to a washing line (see facing page). Blindfold each player by turn, and give them an egg with their name on it in pencil. Spin them around slowly twice, then ask them to attach their egg to the picture as near to where the chicken would have laid it as they can. When everyone has had a turn, the winner is the one whose egg is nearest to the right place.

Tips

You could make a series of seasonal banners for party fun throughout the year: pin the nose (or broom) on the witch for Halloween; the horns on the reindeer for Christmas; the wand on the fairy or the cherry on the cake for birthdays, and so on. The possibilities are almost endless.

Halloween

Pumpkin lanterns

Pumpkin lanterns with ghoulish grins and angular eyes are an essential part of the Halloween tradition and creating the lantern itself can be part of the fun, especially if you have grown the pumpkins yourself. Children will enjoy choosing their own pumpkin and carving out a design with an adult's help. Simply slice the top off the pumpkin, scoop out the flesh and seeds using a metal spoon with sharp sides and then start decorating by carving shapes out of the skin. The scooping is best done by an adult, but children can enjoy carving out the decorative shapes after some instruction on method and safety tips from an adult. The pulp can be saved to make soup or chutney, and the seeds can be served as snacks, sprinkled on salads or flapjacks, or carefully stored for sowing next spring.

Light the finished lanterns and arrange them in a row along the top of a wall or on porch steps until it is time for them to be carefully cradled home. Use three night-lights in each one to give out a warm flickering glow. A cluster of these lanterns in a variety of different designs adds immeasurably to the atmosphere of any gathering, inside or out. But take care to site holes in the lid directly above the candle flames, or you will get roasted pumpkin – and never leave lit lanterns unattended.

It's worth remembering that pumpkin lanterns can be used to bring a warm golden glow to all sorts of autumnal festivities. They can be carved out in any type of decoration – try piercing swirly patterns with a skewer in the style of Mexican tin lanterns, or go for simpler, more geometric patterns such as those shown here. The polka-dot effect was created using an apple corer, which passes easily through the tough skin and flesh of a pumpkin.

A fine crop of pumpkins is a good excuse for a colourful, well-earned autumn party.

Halloween goodie bags

These colourful bags have been designed to go trick-or-treating, and will look great with any spooky costume. They also make perfect goodie bags for a children's Halloween party.

You will need

- Orange fabric cut into pieces approximately 35 x 13cm (14 x 5in). You will need as many pieces as you want bags
- Black felt scraps for decorative motifs
- Scissors
- Sewing thread
- Ribbon: 2 pieces around 35cm (14in) long

To make

- On each piece, start by folding over 1cm (½in) of orange fabric along the longer (35cm/14in) edges, then iron to fix.

- Fold over 2.5cm (1in) on both short ends and iron this fold into place.

- Stitch along both short edges approximately 2cm (¾in) down from the fold – this forms the ribbon channel.

- Cut out some Halloween motifs from the black felt (see page 85 for templates, if you want ideas) and attach each motif with neat running stitch.

- Fold your bag in half, right side to right side, making a bag that is approximately 15 x 11cm (6 x 4in) in size. Snip into the 1cm (½in) folded edge just below the ribbon channel.

- Sew the side seams. Turn the bag right side out and iron.

- Thread a piece of ribbon through both channels, then tie the two ends of ribbon together.

- Starting at the opposite side, thread the second ribbon through both sides and tie the ends together.

- Pull the two ribbons together; this gathers up the top of the bag and will keep precious trick-or-treat sweets safely tucked inside.

Tips

Drawstring fabric bags like this are useful for all sorts of parties or occasions. Choose a colour that suits the festivities and scale up or down in size as required. If you want to make these in a hurry, paint images on the bags with fabric paint instead of sewing on felt motifs.

Spooky silhouettes

Spooky silhouettes and scary shadows are synonymous with October 31, and they're very quick and easy to make. Choose from witches, skeletons, cauldrons, cats, bats or spiders to create a suitably creepy atmosphere.

You will need

- Craft knife
- Pencil
- Thin black card, sugar paper or similar
- Sticky, reusable putty (like Blu-tack™) for attaching silhouettes to windows

To make

- Measure the windows you want to decorate, then cut your card to size.

- If you don't feel confident in your drawing abilities, use the Halloween images provided on page 85 or search the web for ideas. You can scale them up or down on a copier machine.

- On a piece of plain paper, roughly sketch where you want to place each image (this helps to ensure you won't run out of space).

- Draw your images onto the card, then carefully cut out the shape with a craft knife. Remember that you are cutting an outline only. You can stick small detail pieces such as eyes in position on the window with soft tack once your card is in place.

- The cut-out piece that is left after you lift away your shape makes an additional silhouette to attach to a window or wall.

- Backlight your silhouettes by placing a light – such as a candle in a jam jar or your pumpkin lantern – on the window sill and turn out all the other lights in the room. Remember to make sure any candle or lantern is secure and don't ever leave a lit one unattended.

Tips

We used black card but you can just as easily use orange. If the card is not too thick and your craft knife is sharp enough you may want to cut through two layers together – one black and one orange or white – to make the process even quicker.

Birthdays

Vintage birthday banner

There is something very appealing about old fonts and typefaces, and vintage letter cards lend a unique feel to birthday banners. String them together to say 'Happy Birthday!' loud and clear to a loved one.

You will need

- Letter playing cards
- String or ribbon
- Hole punch
- Scissors

To make

• Punch 2 holes at the top of each letter card approximately 1cm (½in) from the side edge.

• Thread the string or ribbon through each card from back to front, then hang your party decoration. Alternatively, pack the threaded piece together and post the banner to an appreciative friend!

Tips

The possibilities are almost limitless – you can use these cards to spell out anything from 'Happy Christmas/Easter' to 'I love you', 'Welcome home', 'Thank you' or someone's name. Vintage letter cards are usually available from auction sites online, but if you don't want to buy a set, simply trace letters from any vintage publication onto plain cards. This will allow you to choose the background colour too. If you do buy a pack of cards, it's worth remembering that individual cards can be used as single-initial birthday cards, so those not used in your banner can be usefully kept for future birthdays.

Pretty piñata

The wonderful thing about homemade piñatas is that you can fill them with whatever you like, as long as the gifts are not too delicate – you can guarantee they'll get a joyous bashing!

You will need

- A large balloon of around 60cm (24in) diameter (available online and from party shops)
- Newspaper cut into strips approximately 5cm (2in) wide
- PVA glue (or flour and water)
- Paint
- Tissue paper sized around 50 x 75cm (20 x 30in); quantity depends on the size of piñata
- String

To make

- Blow up the balloon. Water down the PVA glue or mix up some flour and water to a painting consistency.

- Cover your balloon completely with glue. Methodically dip each piece of newspaper into the glue and place flat onto the balloon. As you work, overlap each piece slightly and smooth out the paper onto the balloon.

- When dry, apply another layer and then repeat once more (3 layers in total) or until you feel it is solid enough. Leave to dry completely.

- Burst the balloon!

- If covering with tissue paper, apply a thin layer of light-coloured paint over the papier maché. Watered-down emulsion is good for this: it dries quickly and is an economical way to cover a large area.

- While the paint is drying, prepare your petals. Fold a sheet of tissue into four lengthways, then fold this piece, accordian style, from left to right. Using a 50 x 75cm (20 x 30in) piece of tissue, you'll end up with a 12.5cm (5in) square. Cut a petal shape from the top folded edge, then cut along the folded edge so that you have 24 individual petals.

- Begin at the base of your papier maché shape. Put a dab of glue on the top two corners of each petal and start attaching them to the papier maché, overlapping them to look like scales. Work around the shape from bottom to top.

- When completely covered, pierce 4 holes at equal distance around the top edge approximately 3cm (1in) from the edge.

- Thread 4 lengths of string (decide on how long you want these) through the holes and double knot each one on the inside to secure. Dab the knots with glue. Tie the 4 lengths together at the top, ready for hanging. Make sure your string is strong enough to hold the weight.

- Fill with sweets and gifts and then hang securely from a ceiling, beam or doorframe.

Tips

This piñata is covered with layers of tissue paper petals, but it is just as easy to decorate with paper fringing using tissue or crêpe paper and following a more traditional pattern. If you have time, you could cover one with scrunched-up tissue paper balls to look like flowers.

For other occasions, you could make a piñata to fit in with your theme: white for a summer wedding, multi-coloured for a child's party, or rich reds and ochres for a Halloween game. A piñata filled with mini eggs and hung from a blossom-covered tree on Easter Sunday would look beautiful and make a great Easter game.

Paper pompoms

These paper decorations are now absolutely on-trend. If you choose the right colours you can transform a room for a party into a stylish and enviable space, and have fun while doing so.

You will need

- Tissue paper – around 6–8 sheets per pompom. We used sheets that measured 50 x 75cm (20 x 30in) for the largest pompom

- Florists' wire (or pipe cleaners)

- Fishing line, invisible thread or cotton to hang

To make

- Working with 6 or 8 sheets of tissue paper at a time, make a 3cm (1in) fold, then pleat – accordian style – along the shortest length, creasing each fold flat.

- Fold the pleated tissue in half and wrap a piece of line around the centre, then twist together to hold the folded paper in shape.

- Use scissors to trim the ends of the tissue into either a rounded or pointed shape.

- Separate the layers, pulling them away from the centre one at a time to pull the pompom into shape.

- Tie some florists' wire or a pipe cleaner to the centre of the pompom to hang it from fishing line or invisible thread. If you want to hang more than one pompom vertically, continue one length of line or thread down through several pompoms, attaching it round each one as you go.

- For smaller pompoms, cut the tissue paper in half or quarters horizontally before you start, then pleat from the shortest edge.

Tips

You could use two colours of tissue in one pompom by alternating the colours before folding. For a really colourful effect, tip the edges with watercolour paint. Different colours and colour approaches can help theme your pompoms to your event – black and orange for Halloween, gold and silver or glittery tissue for a disco, or black and white for a pirate party.

Party bags

Party bags leave a lasting impression of the party, so why not give people something really stylish? You can also make a feature of them as part of the birthday decorations by placing them in a wicker basket.

You will need

- Craft paper
- Binding tape
- Letter stamps (optional)
- Tea-stained luggage tags (see below right).

To make

- Cut out a sheet of paper for each party bag. Our paper sheets measured 12 x 15cm (5 x 6in).

- Fold your paper in half.

- Stitch around 3 sides.

- Insert sweets, gifts or a mixture of small items.

- Cut a length of binding tape slightly longer than double the width of your bag. Fold the tape over the top edge of the bag, sandwiching the bag between the tape, pinning it in place as you work around the top. Stitch the tape into place.

- Make luggage tags by cutting out rectangular pieces of card to the size you want. Write your guests' names (or stamp them on as we did, see right) or a simple 'thank you' on the luggage tags.

- Use a hole punch to make a hole in one corner of the bag and attach the luggage label.

Tea staining labels

To add a vintage feel, you could tea stain your labels. Put a handful of tea bags into a bowl of hot water (it doesn't have to be boiling) and place your paper sheets or card into the water until they are stained. Then lay them flat in a warm place to dry.

Tips

For an easier finish, put the fillings in place then glue all the sides of the bag together, so each bag is completely sealed. Your paper bags could be made from crêpe paper or last year's wrapping paper from your store cupboard. This allows you to theme your bag material to the party. Small versions of these bags made in white crêpe and containing silver-coated chocolates make pretty wedding favours.

Another eye-catching way to display these bags is to attach them to a tree branch standing in a vase or bucket.

Cards, gift wrap and labels

It is far nicer to receive a handmade card than a bought one: it has the added attraction of being personalised and individual, and you may even be saving trees at the same time. The ideas here are also very quick to make. If you have the right materials to hand it is possible to produce a card in minutes, so always squirrel away anything that catches your eye and you'll soon have an archive of materials to work with. Some of the ideas here – such as the playing cards attached with photo corners, or the small card of vintage buttons – are inspirations for using interesting things you already have. Other ideas, such as using woven name tapes saying 'Happy Christmas', are simple but need some planning ahead (the tapes can be ordered from companies that produce name labels for children's clothes and generally take just a few days).

Getting ideas – reuse, recycle

Look out for old books, sheet music and vintage magazines in markets; these are great for card making and for gift wrapping. Search out vintage playing cards too – the decorative sides are often themed and can look wonderful attached to a blank card. If you want something more elaborate, you can stitch together a few cards to spell out a name or word (use cards featuring letters or cut cards into letter shapes) that can then be folded, concertina style, and posted.

As well as making a beautiful decoration, cut-outs such as the ones on pages 38–39 make original cards. Tailor the cut-out to reflect the celebration, and choose a plain paper of any colour or cut from patterned paper. And remember that you can use all your card ideas in miniature for making individualised gift tags or labels.

Continues on page 73

Too precious?

While we are advocating reusing and upcycling, some of your precious vintage paper materials may be too precious to wrap around a gift and give away. This is where technology can really come into its own. Most home printers now scan too, so if you have access to one you can scan an image and print it out, ideally onto tracing or coloured paper. Or you could tea stain some copier paper (see page 68) to look archival. Remember too that your homemade card may not be thrown away by its new owner – homemade cards are often given a third life in a frame.

Sourcing images

Millions of images are available online to download for use on homemade cards or wrapping paper, and many can be reproduced for personal (but not commercial) use. Arts and crafts stores now stock lots of block prints – often as lightweight, plastic stamps that can be slotted on and off an acrylic block, allowing easy interchange. We printed some Christmas cards using these (choosing a small bird and a vintage bauble shape), and it was a great way of producing a large amount of cards very quickly, while keeping that homemade appeal.

Handmade envelopes

The envelope is the first thing the receiver will see, so make something impressive. You can use any kind of paper – old or new – from tracing or baking paper to an old road map, magazine or sheet music. You may need to attach a label so that the address can be read, but there are endless possibilities and best of all, you'll be recycling.

The simplest way to make an envelope is to fold a simple oblong. Measure your card first and add 1cm (½in) to the length and width. Double over the paper so it makes the right shape and stick it along 3 sides. Insert the card and stick the top edge or tape it together. There are two other, slightly more elaborate, ways to make envelopes. The first is to cut out a simple rectangle with pinking shears then stitch all around it (don't forget to insert the card!). The second is to follow the instruction for the party bags on page 68 but include a flap by adding a triangular shape to the top of one side of your bag.

Homemade basics

Craft basics

Whether it's making cushions or throws, wrapping presents or creating cards, having a well-stocked craft kit at the ready can help everything go smoothly. This section tells you what to save for recycling to quickly build the perfect vintage store cupboard.

Our craft kits are a combination of bought stuff – tried-and-tested glues, paints and other products that we know will work well – and goodies saved from here and there, happy in the knowledge that they will be given another life in some creative project or other. We save everything, from pretty wrapping paper (larger areas only and with the creases ironed out where necessary) to rubber bands and

ribbons from presents or bouquets of flowers, and even the coloured cotton tape from the heavy paper bags that are increasingly given away in shops instead of plastic bags. Not having to hunt around the house to locate the right type of glue, roll of sticky tape and so on will allow your creativity full rein, ensuring that your project will turn out the best it can possibly be, so these pages list a few suggestions for building a good, general craft kit.

Saving items for recycling can be problematic in terms of storage, but we've found that a large drawer works really well, especially when it contains boxes or dividers to keep everything organised. Also useful are mini chests of drawers made from wood or cardboard that can be stacked up alongside or on top of one another and added to when required. But as with the projects, be creative. You might prefer something more idiosyncratic to contain your kit, such as a sturdy reclaimed wicker laundry basket with old biscuit tins housing all the bits inside, or a series of lovely old leather suitcases of varying sizes. The important thing is to have a system that works efficiently and looks pleasing into the bargain.

The Homemade craft kit

- Different types of glue for paper, fabric and wood, and super-glue for fiddly items
- Sticky tape and double-sided tape
- Masking tape

- Roll of brown parcel paper
- Plain white adhesive labels of various sizes
- Lead pencils
- Coloured crayons
- Set of felt pens
- Fountain pen and coloured inks
- Staple gun
- Drawing pins
- Tacks
- Hammer
- Paper (coloured and white)
- Scissors (small and large)
- Pinking shears
- Ribbons
- Fabric scraps
- Yarn scraps
- Buttons

For wrapping presents
- Brown parcel paper
- Newsprint and magazine paper

- Lining paper (from a wallpaper or DIY store)
- Tissue paper in a variety of colours
- Rescued/reused wrapping paper sorted into larger pieces for reuse and smaller pieces for strips and borders (if you can find time to iron out creases, the paper will look much better)
- String
- Raffia
- Reels of new ribbon in one or two key colours. Red, for example, can perk up newsprint or brown paper, and silver is good for use with tissue paper or even coloured magazine pages
- Silver paint, which is good for painting stars, names and other adornments
- Silver and gold pens
- Pompoms and other embellishments that will perk up plainer wrapping
- Old-fashioned brown paper luggage labels in various sizes or scraps of cardboard for making your own labels
- Dried leaves and flowers

And for painting projects
- Primer/undercoat for dark and light colours
- Outdoor and indoor eggshell paint: preferably water-based for ease of use and lower chemical content
- White spirit: for cleaning brushes if using oil-based paints
- Brushes in various sizes, from 5–7.5cm (2–3in) wide for covering larger areas to pointed artists' brushes for handpainting
- Fabric paints and/or fabric crayons
- Erasable pencil/chalk for marking out projects

Sewing basics

This section tells you what kind of things to keep in your sewing kit, in order to make the projects from this book and anything else you're likely to want to sew. It also shows you how to sew the four most useful stitches.

It is good to have two sewing kits: one can be small and portable, containing the bare essentials (needles, thread, safety pins and a spare button or two) that you keep in a handbag and use for mending on the go, and the other much more extensive – based at home and used for larger projects, such as those in this book.

The following items are recommended for the larger kit.

The sewing kit

- At least two pairs of sharp scissors: small, very sharp embroidery scissors (good for unpicking) and a good-quality pair of fabric shears. By including both pairs of scissors, you are ensuring that the fabric scissors will last a long time.
- Pinking shears for making zig-zag edges to hems (less likely to fray) and cutting fabrics, such as felt, in an attractive way.
- Pins stuck in a pretty pincushion, handmade if possible, though magnetic pin holders are also available. Many people find quilting pins with coloured heads easier to handle, and they are certainly easier to see, making it less likely

that you will leave pins in place on a finished item. Larger-headed pins are particularly useful when working with knitting or crochet.
- Hand-sewing needles in various sizes, including thicker darning needles for working with thicker thread or wool.
- Safety pins, fastened together for safety and convenience.
- Tailor's chalk for marking out patterns (this washes or brushes out easily).
- Cotton thread in various colours; keep commonly used colours in longer reels.
- Tape measure in imperial and metric.
- Poppers and hooks and eyes for fastening.
- Fusible fabric, such as Bondaweb.
- Button box containing buttons of all shapes, colours and sizes.
- Rag bag full of scraps and smaller pieces of fabric that you have saved up over the years.
- Steam iron for pressing fabric before, during and after making up.

Non-essentials, but useful

- Basic sewing machine (not essential but certainly useful) and a variety of sewing machine needles.
- Thimble, especially if you get sore fingers and thumbs.
- Seam ripper/unpicker.
- Ruler to provide a more solid edge than a tape measure.
- Embroidery threads in all colours.
- Tapestry wool for embellishments.

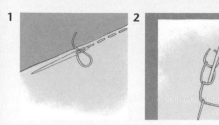
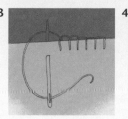
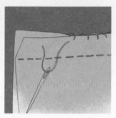

1 **2** **3** **4**

Basic stitches used in this book

Most of the instructions below are based on those supplied on the website of the Embroiderer's Guild (www. embroiderersguild.com/stitch/stitches). There are also some superb YouTube entries, some of which show the creation of the stitches very clearly, accompanied by music.

1 Running stitch

Pass the needle in and out of the fabric, making sure that the surface stitches are of equal length. The stitches on the underside should be of equal length to one another, but half the size or less than the upper stitches.

2 Chain stitch

Having pulled the needle through the fabric, insert the needle next to where it emerged and bring the point out a short distance away. Pull the thread around the needle, keeping it under the needle's point, and pull through the fabric to create a looped stitch. Holding down the loop, repeat to make a series of linked chains.

3 Blanket stitch

Push the needle up through the fabric a short way from the edge, hooking the rest of the thread around the top of the needle. Pull the needle through the fabric, keeping

the lower thread out of the way so the thread forms a loop around the edge of the fabric. Repeat to create a line of linked stitches along the fabric edge.

4 Over stitch

This stitch is worked from the right side and is often used to join together pieces of fabric, or as an alternative to blanket stitch to prevent fraying. Place the pieces of work together with wrong sides facing, then bring the needle up through both layers from the underside. Repeat, always bringing the needle from the underside of the work. The thread binds together the two layers of fabric. Over stitch is especially useful for joining the fabric of a stuffed toy.

Knitting basics

One of the best things about knitting is that you need very little in the way of equipment, especially when knitting simple items such as gloves and scarves. The real skill lies in choosing yarns and getting to know your preferred style and tension.

By far the best way to learn knitting is one-on-one from a more experienced friend or relative. But there are also many groups and drop-in 'clinics' around, both formal and informal, where the sociable side of craft also comes into play. For further information on courses, see the Directory on pages 88–90. The excellent website www.domiknitrix.com includes a gallery of pictures to help you learn various stitches, including mattress stitch.

The knitting kit

- A selection of knitting needles: the ones most commonly used are size 2.75mm (UK size 12; US size 2), 3.25mm (UK size 10; US size 3), 4.5mm (UK size 7; US size 7) and 6.5mm (UK size 3; US size 10½).
- Various crochet hooks of different sizes, including 2mm and 2.5mm.
- Tape measure.
- Small sharp scissors.
- Pencil and paper.
- Stitch holder (at least one, for holding stitches when changing needles).
- Safety pins of various sizes.
- Needle gauge: for checking needle sizes.
- Circular needles: for making socks and gloves.
- Darning needles: for sewing flat pieces of knitting together.
- Button box of buttons.
- Selection of small scraps of knitting yarn for embroidery and darning.

Choosing yarn

Different yarns give different results: smooth and silky or rough and hairy. Long filaments create a different effect compared to short ones – compare the difference between an item made with mohair and one made with a tightly twisted yarn. Take this into account when choosing yarn for a project.

Whatever yarn you choose, try to make it the best possible quality. After all the time and love you put into making something, you don't want it to look tired, misshapen and bobbly after only one wash. Numerous companies (see the Directory, pages 88–90) make beautiful ranges of pure and mixed yarn and have pure wool that washes well and feels soft and wearable.

Yarn usually comes in 50g (2oz) balls but, for economy, try to find yarn on large hanks, or larger still 500g (1lb 2oz) cones, which are a cheaper option when buying new.

Quite often yarn is reduced if it is an odd dye lot (see 'Notes for knitters', right) and this is worth buying to add to your store when knitting or crocheting things that use small quantities.

The make-do-and-mend mentality of the post-war generation meant it was common for people to unravel and re-knit their jerseys, steaming the wool to take out the kinks. While we wouldn't advocate this as essential, it certainly makes sense financially, provided you have time. It might be worth considering the next time your child outgrows a favourite hand-knit or you see an item made from a lovely yarn but don't like the garment style.

Knitting terms

In the UK and USA, yarns are referred to by different terms:

UK	US
4-ply	Sportweight
Double knit	Worsted
Aran	Fisherman or medium weight
Chunky	Bulky

Notes for knitters

- *Always* work a tension swatch, no matter how little time you have. Then check it against the pattern and change your needles accordingly if necessary.
- The knitting tensions quoted on the patterns in this book are a guide only. Every knitter has a natural personal tension, which may be tight or loose.
- To check your tension, knit a square to the size given in the pattern and using the stitch from the pattern. When the square is complete, lay it on a flat surface and, using a tape measure, count the number of stitches and then the number of rows.
- If you have more stitches or rows than the tension indicated, use slightly smaller needles. If you have fewer stitches or rows, try using larger needles.

- The difference in tension also means that some knitters may use more or less yarn than that quoted. Once you know whether your tension is slightly tight or loose, adjust your yarn allowance slightly.
- If buying more than one ball of the same-coloured yarn, make sure they all have the same batch number – this is printed on the ball band. Although balls of yarn may look the same to the naked eye, if you use the same colour from different dye batches, it will always show on the finished piece and spoil the uniform effect.
- When it's time to put your knitting away, pop a cork on the end of your needles to stop the stitches falling off.
- Never leave your knitting in the middle of a row or there may be an obviously larger stitch in the middle once it is finished.

Abbreviations used

cont	continue
col	colour
dec	decrease/decreasing
inc	increase/increasing
k	knit
MC	main colour
p	purl
rep	repeat
RS	right side
st st	stocking stitch
st/sts	stitches
tog	together

Patterns and templates

The patterns we have used are very simple and, in most cases, consist of a hard outline with a dotted line if there is a fold or a line of stitching. Cut as many pieces as you need for your projects, remembering that material sometimes needs to be doubled and/or placed on a fold. If you are using the pattern in the same size as here, simply trace the outline plus any other detailing onto tracing or baking paper. Then pin the paper onto the fabric and cut around the shape, cutting through the fabric and paper (if this is the first time you have used the pattern). If you want to transfer any extra markings to the fabric, use dressmaker's chalk, which will wash out.

Felt decorations

See project on page 12
Enlarge patterns to around 150%
for tree decorations

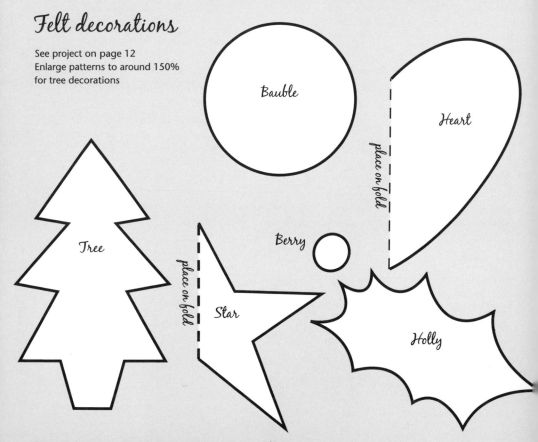

Bauble

Heart

place on fold

Tree

Berry

place on fold

Star

Holly

felt decorations continued

See Christmas tree felt decoration project on page 12
Use pattern at the same size as here

Pretty piñata

See project on page 64
Enlarge pattern to around 300% to reach the size required

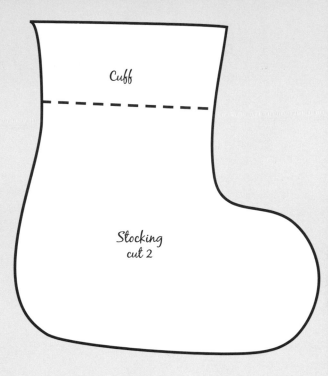

Cuff

Stocking
cut 2

Petal
cut enough to
cover your balloon

Christmas stocking

See project on page 32
Enlarge patterns to suit the size of your stocking

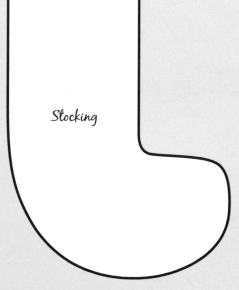

Stocking

Bird

Valentine paper cut-outs

See project on page 38
Resize patterns to suit your project

Je t'aime

Valentine heart

See projects on page 36–40
Enlarge pattern to your required size

Valentine heart

Easter decorations

See projects on pages 46–48
Enlarge patterns to around 200% for the Easter bird decorations and the Easter egg bunting

Easter chick

Easter egg

Halloween templates

See projects on pages 54–58
Resize patterns to suit your requirements

Moon

Witch

Spider

Cat

Directory

Paints and papers

Shops and mail-order

EarthBorn Paints
T 01928 734171 for stockists
www.earthbornpaints.co.uk
One of the highest eco-rated
UK paint companies.

Farrow & Ball
T 01202 876141 for stockists
www.farrow-ball.com
Farrow & Ball do all their
luscious colours in indoor
and outdoor eggshell.

JustWipe
T 01606 836179
www.justwipe.co.uk
Large collection of oilcloths.

Oilcloth UK
www.oilcloth.co.uk
Wide choice of oilcloths,
including colourful, gaudy
Mexican designs.

Papers & Paints
T 020 7352 8626
www.papers-paints.co.uk
Check out their 'Historical'

range for unusual shades that
would suit both period and
modern styles.

Russell and Chapple
68 Drury Lane, London
WC2B 5SP
T 020 7836 7521
www.russellandchapple.co.uk
Old-fashioned, extremely
efficient arts supplier of
everything from canvas and
scrim cloth to professional
painting supplies.

Shepherd's Bookbinders
76 Southampton Row,
London WC1B 4AR
T 020 7831 1151
www.bookbinding.co.uk
One of the best sources of
unusual papers and cards.

Websites

www.pinterest.com
Pinterest is a virtual pinboard
to organise and share
pictures of the things you
make or love. it's great for
constructing virtual mood
boards.

Sewing

Useful organisations

**Northern Ireland
Embroidery Guild**
www.nieg.org.uk
Excellent workshops in
embroidery, felting and
beadwork, in various venues
in the UK.

Royal School of Needlework
Hampton Court Palace,
East Molesey, Surrey KT8 9AU
T 020 3166 6932
www.royal-needlework.co.uk
Charity that offers a wide
range of courses and
wonderful tours of their
needlework collection, in
the genteel surroundings of
Hampton Court Palace.

Sewing shops and mail-order suppliers

The Cloth House
47 Berwick Street,
London W1F 8SJ
T 020 7437 5155
www.clothhouse.com

Vintage trimmings and ribbons alongside a huge range of natural fabrics.

The Cloth Shop
290 Portobello Road,
London W10 5TE
T 020 8968 6001
www.theclothshop.net

The Cotton Patch
1285 Stratford Road, Hall Green, Birmingham B28 9AJ
T 0121 702 2840
www.cottonpatch.co.uk
Fantastic shop and website specialising in patchwork.

Duttons for Buttons
Oxford Street, Harrogate,
North Yorkshire HG1 1QE
T 01423 502092
www.duttonsforbuttons.co.uk
Wonderful shop bursting with all manner of buttons.

Exeter Sewing Machine Company
7 Heavitree Road, Exeter,
Devon EX1 2LD
T 01392 275660
www.exetersewing.co.uk
Great source of thread, fabric and general supplies.

I Knit London
106 Lower Marsh, Waterloo,
London SE1 7AB
T 020 7261 1338
www.iknit.org.uk

In-Fabrics
12 Old Bridge,
Haverfordwest,
Pembrokeshire SA61 2ET
T 01437 769164
www.in-fabrics.com
More than 2,000 rolls of fabric in stock!

Kleins
5 Noel Street,
London W1F 8GD
T 020 7437 6162
www.kleins.co.uk
Chaos reigns in this Soho institution, but chances are they will have what you want …plus they do mail order.

Liberty
Regent Street,
London W1B 5AH
T 020 7734 1234
www.liberty.co.uk
This huge, wonderful shop is an all-time classic – both the haberdashery and furnishing departments are brilliant, and very inspiring.

MacCulloch and Wallis
25–26 Dering Street,
London W1S 1AT
T 020 7629 0311
www.macculloch-wallis.co.uk
Old-fashioned fabric shop selling all sorts of dress trimmings and materials, as well as good haberdashery supplies.

Mandors
131 East Claremont Street,
Edinburgh EH7 4JA
T 0131 558 3888
www.mandors.co.uk
Mandors have a great supply of dressmaking and furnishing materials.

Millie Moon Shop
24–25 Catherine Hill,
Frome, Somerset BA11 1BY
T 01373 464650
www.milliemoonshop.co.uk
Haberdashery boutique and sewing school.

Millers Creativity Shop
28 Stockwell Street,
Glasgow G1 4RT
T 0141 553 1660
www.millers-art.co.uk
Creative superstore with plenty of sewing equipment.

Olicana Textiles Ltd
Brook Mills, Crimble,
Slaithwaite, Huddersfield HD7
T 01484 847666
www.olicana.co.uk

Sew Creative
97–99 King Street,
Cambridge CB1 1LD
T 01223 350691
www.sewcreative.co.uk
Suppliers of Pfaff and Singer sewing machines along with a good range of yarn and fabric.

The Sewing Bee
52 Hillfoot Street, Dunoon,
Argyll, Scotland PA23 7DT
T 01369 706879
www.thesewingbee.co.uk
Gorgeous bijou haberdashers.

Singer and Pfaff Sewing Centre
2 Queen Street, Penzance,
Cornwall TR18 4BJ
T 01736 363457
www.iriss.co.uk
Supplier of sewing machines
with a good range of fabrics.

Samuel Taylor
10 Central Road,
Leeds LS1 6DE
T 0113 245 9737
www.clickoncrafts.co.uk
Old-fashioned haberdasher
with a modern online shop.

St Jude's Fabrics
T 01603 662951
www.stjudesfabrics.co.uk
St Jude's works with an
eclectic range of artists to
produce original printed
fabrics that form a brilliant
basis for almost anything.

VV Rouleaux
www.vvrouleaux.com
Famous ribbon specialists
with fabulous selection in
many colours and widths.
See website for branches in
England and Scotland.

Sewing websites

www.betsyrosspatterns.com
Easy-to-follow sewing
patterns to order online.

www.fitzpatterns.com
Fashionably funky patterns to
download, many for free.

www.gloriouscolor.com
American quilter's site that
ships internationally.

www.hiplinemedia.com
Los Angeles-based group of
stitchers who produce great
instructional DVDs.

www.opheliabutton.co.uk
Jewellery and other treasures
made from beautiful vintage
buttons.

www.sewing.org
Instructions on a wide
range of techniques,
including fashion sewing
and creating pet clothes.

www.sewmamasew.com
Fun modern cotton fabrics
and patterns from indie
designers in Oregon, USA.

www.vpll.org
Fascinating pattern library
featuring designs from
1840 to 1950 with vintage
publications too.

Sewing books

Colourful Stitchery by Kristin
Nicholas (Storey Books).
Wonderful, exuberant
embroidery that is sure to
inspire and delight.

*Mary Thomas's Dictionary of
Embroidery Stitches* by Mary
Thomas (Caxton Editions).
A real classic.

Knitting and crochet

Useful organisations

Knitting and Crochet Guild
www.kcguild.org.uk
An amazing organisation
set up to promote and
encourage the crafts of
hand knitting, machine
knitting and crochet. Aimed
at makers that are also
interested in the history of
knitting and crochet, it is
full of information and links
to archival material. It runs
classes too.

UK Hand Knitting Association
www.ukhandknitting.com
A mine of information on
classes, knitting groups,
shows and shops.

Victoria and Albert Museum
Cromwell Road,
London SW7 2RL
T 020 7942 2000
www.vam.ac.uk
Has a great website – type
'knitting' into the search
box for everything from the
history of knitting to the
best shops, free patterns and
knitting blogs.

Knitting and crochet classes

Learning from other people
is the best way to start any
new craft – either one-on-one
with a friend or in a group
of local people interested in
extending their skills. There
are also various 'knitting
gurus' offering tailor-made
classes for individuals or
groups. And don't forget
YouTube!

Ros Badger, one of the
authors of this book, offers
knitting lessons in South
London (www.rosbadger.
com) and her book *Instant
Expert: Knitting* is full of
inspirational photographs.
Read her blog at **www.
rosbadger.blogspot.co.uk**
and follow her on Twitter:
@rosbadger.

Knitting shops and mail-order suppliers

Get Knitted
39 Brislington Hill, Brislington,
Bristol BS4 5BE
www.getknitted.com
Great yarns and patterns.

Loop
15 Camden Passage,
London N1 8EA
T 020 7288 1160
www.loopknitting.com
Fine-looking shop stuffed
with lovely candy-coloured
yarns. You can also drop in
for emergency knitting advice
or enrol in lunchtime classes.

Purlescence Ltd
Boston House,
Downsview Road,
Wantage,
Oxfordshire OX12 9YF
www.purlescence.co.uk
Purlescence has a modern
take on all things knitting.

Stash Yarns
213 Upper Richmond Road,
London SW15 6SQ
T 020 8246 6666
www.stashyarns.co.uk
Another great shop selling
yarns from around the world.

Knitting websites

www.angelyarns.com

This site claims to be Europe's
largest online yarn store, and
it certainly does have a huge
number of yarns!

www.castoff.info
Radical knitting website that
arranges adventurous knitting
meetings and workshops in
unusual public settings.

www.colinette.com
An unusual range of hand-
dyed yarns in many different
colour combinations.

www.cornishorganicwool.
co.uk
This company produces
organically certified yarns,
in pure wool and a wool/
alpaca mix. All the wool is
spun in Scotland at a mill
powered by a water wheel
and hand dyed.

www.domiknitrix.com
Great for fun but straight-
talking help on knocking your
knitting into shape.

www.kangaroo.uk.com
This site provides a world-
wide mail-order service for
knitting kits, patterns, yarns
and needles.

www.knitty.com
An amazing US-based
resource for knitters, offering

free patterns, articles and technical advice for novices and experienced knitters alike – all spooled out with welcome warmth and humour in an online periodical magazine format.

www.laughinghens.com
Online wool store with a really good range of patterns, yarns (including organic), threads, kits, accessories and books.

www.louet.com
This US firm produces finest-quality Euroflax linen in an inspiring range of colours. They also sell exotic fibres, from yak to silk.

www.shetlandwoolbrokers.co.uk
This company sources wool from over 700 of Shetland's crofters and farmers.

www.mazzmatazz.co.uk
Site of the original 'rebel knitter' who designed cuddly versions of *Doctor Who* villains.

www.nexstitch.com
Easy-to-read crochet patterns for ponchos, shawls and other accessories – even bikinis.

www.ravelry.com

Like Facebook for knitters – you can share projects, tips and chat with like-minded fellow knitters.

www.simplysockyarn.com
American company with a great list of yarns from all the top producers.

www.stitchnbitch.org
For local group knitting and general craft-club gossip while you knit, or look at your local press and craft/art shop windows. Stitchnbitch also produce books with fun, unusual patterns.

www.texere.co.uk
All kinds of yarn, plus chenille, metallic yarns and embroidery thread.

www.theknittinghut.com

www.yarnstorm.blogs.com
The wonderful website of Jane Brocket, who really put sewing, knitting and patchwork back on the map. Her book, *The Gentle Art of Domesticity,* is also a delight.

www.ysolda.com
Website of lovely young Scottish knitter.

Knitting books

Complete Guide to Knitting and Crochet by Nicki Trench (Parragon).
Great illustrations and an informative, easy-to-follow style of writing. The book includes plenty of simple but interesting projects that even beginners can master.

The Crochet Answer Book by Edie Eckman (Storey).
A useful addition to your crochet library.

Kyuuto! Japanese Crafts: Lacy Crochet (Chronicle Books).
Quirky patterns with a Japanese view on crochet.

General sites and suppliers

Some of these are places where we buy items we love, others (the more expensive among them) are where we go to get inspired. Exposing yourself to as much good-quality and beautiful material, whether it is clothes or furniture or food, is great for getting the mind going and thinking of your own ideas to create. It's not plagiarism – slavish copying is definitely not on the agenda – it's more letting one person's ideas and creativity inspire your own.

Mary Mathieson
An artist with a special interest in working with flowers, who did some of the illustrations and made many of the projects in this book. She can be contacted on **T** 07940 919622.

www.caravanstyle.com
Stylist Emily Chalmers set up this gorgeous shop specialising in vintage thrift in the most stylish way possible.

www.charlenemullen.com
Incredibly talented textile designer specialising in cushions and homeware – rather expensive, but handmade using the most sumptuous fabrics and a real inspiration.

www.designspongeonline.com
Lovely things noticed and described with an observant and original eye.

www.etsy.com
The place to sell all your homemade craft items, to keen buyers from around the world.

www.frankworks.eu
British alternative applied arts and contemporary craft – books and badges, jewellery and stationery, textiles, prints, ceramics and lighting that are often handmade, original, and often quirky.

www.fredbare.co.uk
For some of the most stylish hats in town. The lovely shop at 118 Columbia Road, London E2 7RG (01904 624579) is usually only open on Sundays so ring or email via the website.

www.helpyourshelf.co.uk
Lovely website and shop full of unique and stylish objects.

www.vialiivia.blogspot.co.uk
You don't need to speak Finnish to appreciate this photographer's blog with its sensitive, beautiful photographs, documenting the homely (and naturally stylish) domestic life of Liivian and her young daughter. Her fellow Scandinavian's blog, Vintage Living at www.myblogvintageliving.blogspot.com, is similarly inspiring.

www.papastour.com
Scottish arts and crafts with lots of lovely things plus a hideaway to rent.

www.pedlars.co.uk
Great, fun, original items, including many that aid creativity – old printers' blocks, vintage tins and reclaimed plant pots, old-fashioned cleaning equipment, sticky tape dispensers and so on.

www.re-foundobjects.co.uk
'Re' stands for 'recycled, restored, reused' – and their website and shop are bristling with original finds and new ways to use old objects and fabrics, which can't help but be inspiring. Their store is in Bishops Yard, Main Street, Corbridge, Northumberland NE45 5LA.

www.squintlimited.com
For heavenly, somewhat pricey original items. Great for inspiring your own homespun versions.

www.yarnstorm.blogs.com
The creation of the fantastically inspiring and prolific Jane Brocket, who knits, patchworks, cooks and gardens and posts her creations online. This is one of the first and best of the many craft websites, including knitting, sewing, embroidery and cake baking!

Index

Acknowledgements

I would like to thank my husband Benjamin J Murphy for his perfectionist's eye and dedication – his photographs have made this book truly beautiful. Also Mary Mathieson for her wonderful illustrations, and for contributing to various projects throughout the book. Hanks (sic) also to my very creative teenage daughters for their advice and quirkiness.

Huge thanks are also due to Jane Turnbull, a brilliant agent, who believed in this idea from the start; Denise Bates for the original commission and all at HarperCollins for their hard work, particularly Elen Jones for championing this new edition. Thanks to Sarah Tomley for her excellent editing skills and to Tracy Killick for designing such a beautiful book.

I would also like to thank Piers Feltham, Chiara Menage and Caddy and Chris Wilmot-Sitwell for allowing us to take photographs in their gardens.

Thank you also to the many other people who have contributed with their own imaginative ideas to this book – Monica McMillan, Katy Jaffey, Rebecca Tanqueray, Caddy Wilmot-Sitwell and Kristin Perers among others. Also to all the children who have travelled through my sewing clubs and who continue to inspire me with their never-ending inventive interpretations of my ideas.

Thank you to my mum Ruth Badger for teaching me how to sew when I was very young, and her sister Joan Kenwright who, together with my mum, spent hours 'on the sewing machine' throughout my childhood. Also thanks to my grandmother Mary Elizabeth Hunter for teaching me how to crochet when I was seven years old.

Lastly, to my dearest friend Elspeth Thompson whose reputation as a writer and all-round dedication to artistry meant we were commissioned to make *Homemade: Gorgeous Things to Make with Love* back in 2008. Her influence, vision and beauty will stay with me always.

Ros Badger

Also available...

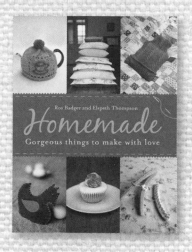

Homemade: **Gorgeous Things to Make with Love**

Over 100 ideas for beautiful and unique things to make throughout the year, from cordials, cupcakes and crocheted coat-hangers to summer bunting and Christmas decorations. Includes beautiful photography, practical step-by-step methods and expert hints and tips.

ISBN 9780007360574

Homemade **Knit, Sew & Crochet**

Learn to make 25 fun and simple knitting, sewing and crochet projects that will add individuality to your home and wardrobe. Complete with step-by-step instructions and beautiful photography, this book is perfect for beginners.

ISBN 9780007489534

Collins